To Catherine, who loves the seaside
and especially the puffins!

S.B.

First published in 2019 by Nosy Crow Ltd
The Crow's Nest, 14 Baden Place, Crosby Row
London SE1 1YW
www.nosycrow.com

ISBN 978 1 78800 250 9

Text © Nosy Crow 2019
Illustrations © Sebastien Braun 2019

The right of Nosy Crow to be identified as the author and Sebastien Braun
to be identified as the illustrator of this work has been asserted.

A CIP catalogue record for this book is available from the British Library.

Printed in China

Papers used by Nosy Crow are made from wood grown in sustainable forests.

1 3 5 7 9 8 6 4 2

LOOK AND SAY
WHAT YOU SEE
AT THE SEASIDE

Sebastien Braun

Have you ever been to the seaside? There's usually a lot to see and it's especially great if you can visit when the sun is shining.

Can you see . . . ?

ice cream   kite   deckchair   umbrella

What do you like to do at the beach?

beach ball picnic suncream sun hat dog

The beach is the perfect place to practise building sandcastles.

Can you see . . . ?

seaweed   bucket   spade   fossil

You can decorate them with things
that you find washed up on the shore.

sandcastle   seashell   driftwood   feather   pebbles

Look at all the people splashing around in the water!

Can you see . . . ?

rubber ring   turnstone   armbands   razor shell

Some are using snorkels so
they can breathe underwater!

sanderling   snorkel   surfer   lifeguard   mermaid's purse

It's busy by the harbour with boats sailing in and out. There are a lot of hungry seagulls, too.

Can you see . . . ?

yacht   lighthouse   fishing rod   seagull

bench   dinghy   speedboat   porpoise   cat

From the top of the cliffs, there's a great view of the seaside below. It's often very windy, so hold on to your hat!

The paraglider loves the wind as it takes him flying over the sea.

Can you see . . . ?

tree   kayak   tern   cave

signpost   sheep   paraglider   climber   kittiwake

The rock pools are full of animals.
Some are bright and colourful,
but some blend in to the rocks
and don't look like animals at all!

Can you
see . . . ?

sea anemone

shore crab

prawn

sea urchin

You have to look closely
to see the world underwater.

mussels   whelk   limpets   periwinkle   hermit crab

Further out at sea, fishing boats are catching
fish. It can be slippery on deck – especially
when there's a storm.

Can you
see . . . ?

fishing net

seal pup

lifebelt

wellington boot

How many seals can you count on the rocks?

buoy   albatross   flag   lobster pot   seal

An estuary is where a river meets the sea and they're brilliant places to go birdwatching.

Can you
see . . . ?   heron   curlew   oystercatcher   lapwing

Most birds that live here
have long legs for wading
in the water.

otter   reeds   dragonfly   coot   caterpillar

Sand dunes are big hills of sand and you'll often find them at the seaside.

Can you see . . .?

butterfly   buzzard   beetle   stoat

If you look closely, you might
see a lot of tiny animals hiding
in the sand.

spider   bee   grass snake   sand lizard   rabbit

Many animals live completely under the water, so they spend all their time swimming. Some have special gills to help them breathe.

Can you see . . . ?

dolphin   whale   basking shark   squid

How many legs does
the octopus have?

jellyfish   scuba diver   sponge   eel   octopus

Some creatures even live right at the bottom of the sea. Can you see any animals that are shaped like stars?

Can you see . . .?

coral   lobster   blenny   stickleback

Coral might look like a
plant, but it's actually
an animal, too!

cuttlefish   starfish   anchor   seahorse   flatfish

Sometimes around the coast you'll
see high walls of rock called cliffs.

Can you
see . . . ?

puffin   nest   chick   egg

Some birds make their nests on the clifftops – it can be very noisy and smelly!

thistle   thrift   cormorant   gannet   gorse

LOOK AND SAY
WHAT YOU SEE
AT THE SEASIDE